THIS CANDLEWICK BOOK BELONGS TO:

This book is a conversation between a granddad and his grandson. When the granddad speaks, it looks **like this,** and when the grandson speaks, it looks *like this.*

Text copyright © 2004 by Vivian French
Illustrations copyright © 2004 by Alison Bartlett

First paperback edition 2006

Library of Congress Catologing-in-Publication Data is available.

Library of Congress Catalog Card Number 2003069563

ISBN-10 0-7636-2184-6 (hardcover)
ISBN-13 978-0-7636-2184-1 (hardcover)
ISBN-10 0-7636-3177-9 (paperback)
ISBN-13 978-0-7636-3177-2 (paperback)

10 9 8 7 6 5 4 3 2 1

Printed in China

This book was typeset in Journal and Tree-Boxelder.
The illustrations were done in acrylic.

Candlewick Press
2067 Massachusetts Avenue
Cambridge, Massachusetts 02140

visit us at www.candlewick.com

For John Joe
V. F.

For Lucie, Steve,
Oscar, and
Harry—much love
A. B.

T. REX

VIVIAN FRENCH

illustrated by
ALISON BARTLETT

THIS WAY TO THE
T. REX EXHIBITION

CANDLEWICK PRESS
CAMBRIDGE, MASSACHUSETTS

It began with an egg!

What size was
the egg?

The egg was as big as your head . . . maybe.
Don't you know? Why don't you know?

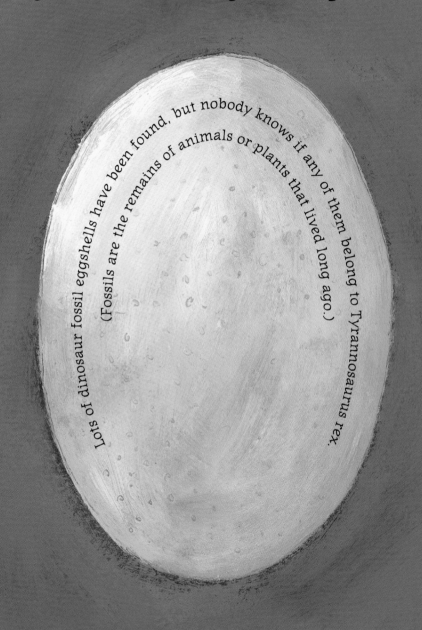

Lots of dinosaur fossil eggshells have been found, but nobody knows if any of them belong to Tyrannosaurus rex. (Fossils are the remains of animals or plants that lived long ago.)

It was millions and millions of years ago!

Was the egg in a nest?
Was the nest in a tree?

8

The egg was buried in sand . . .
maybe.

The way fossil eggshells lie suggests
they have been resting on a sandy base.

Don't you know? Why don't you know?
It was millions and millions of years ago!

And the sun beamed down, and the sand
grew hot. And the egg cracked open.
And what came out? A tiny dinosaur.
A carnosaur. Tyrannosaur—
TYRANNOSAURUS REX!

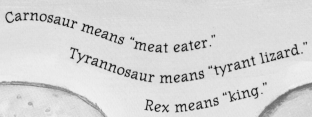

Carnosaur means "meat eater."
Tyrannosaur means "tyrant lizard."
Rex means "king."

And how did he grow?
Or don't you know?

It was millions and
millions of years ago!

There was danger there. Wherever he went
were carnosaurs—eaters of meat—
walking and stalking and sniffing around.

ADULT GORGOSAURUS

ADULT ALBERTOSAURUS

There were lots of big meat-eating dinosaurs,
including Gorgosaurus and Albertosaurus.

Young dinosaurs would have had to watch out.

An adult Tyrannosaurus rex was forty feet long and twenty feet high.

And anything moving might have been LUNCH! Munch! Crunch!

ADULT T. REX

It weighed more than seven tons.

Females were bigger than males.

But he ducked and
he dived and he ate
and he grew.

With his two strong legs
and dagger-clawed toes,

No one knows what kind of noise
Tyrannosaurus rex might have made.

14

and his scaly skin and his hungry
eyes and his terrible teeth . . .

Small pieces of fossilized skin have been found, but
we have no idea what color dinosaurs really were.

T. rex had sixty teeth, which were each up to six inches long. They had edges like saws — perfect for tearing and ripping hides.

How were his teeth, his terrible teeth?
Were they sharp? Were they long?
Were they terribly strong?

16

Did he rip and tear as he charged and leapt,
as he thundered after his panicking prey?

Maybe yes,
or maybe no—
it was millions and millions of years ago.

He MIGHT have leapt and lunged and ripped,
or he MIGHT have wandered for miles and miles,
sniffing the air for the smell of flesh,
flesh that was dying or flesh that was dead—
he might have hunted for secondhand prey,
a scavenger clearing
the dead away.

The fossil skulls of carnosaurs like T. rex show they had
very sensitive nostrils and a good sense of smell.

19

Did he hunt with his friends?
Did he hunt with his mate?

No one knows how fast Tyrannosaurus rex would have moved. Scientists sometimes guess from tracks, but only a single tyrannosaur fossil footprint has been found. (So far.)

Tyrannosaurus rex skeletons

are usually found on their own.

He probably hunted and ate alone,
but then again—we don't really know.

It was millions and millions of years ago. . . .

You keep saying that, but I want to know.
How can I know what's REALLY true?

The answer is that it's up to you —
you can look at those dinosaur bones.

Now, do YOU think he walked or ran?
How do you think he found his food?

Did he roar? Did he growl?
Did he rumble and purr?

How did he live and how did he die?

Did he care for his babies or leave them alone?

Maybe one day we'll REALLY know. . . .
Maybe we'll know what's really true.

There is so much we don't know about dinosaurs yet. Only more discoveries will help us find the answers. Scientists who study dinosaurs are called paleontologists. (Will that be you?)

The person to tell us might just be YOU!

INDEX

Look up the pages to find out about all these T. rex things. Don't forget to look at all the kinds of words—**this kind**, *this kind*, and this kind.

About the Author

Vivian French lives in Edinburgh, Scotland, and has written dozens of books. "I've always loved dinosaurs," she says, "and T. rex in particular—it's the SIZE! The fact we know so little about them fascinates me. In my lifetime the experts have changed their minds many times over. Maybe T. rex will turn out to be a dragon!"

About the Illustrator

Alison Bartlett lives in Bath, England, with her son, Joel. Together they have searched for dinosaur fossils but have yet to find one. Instead, they regularly make dinosaur models and have even built a dinosaur land, with the help of Emma, their neighbor.

About T. rex

The only thing we know for sure about Tyrannosaurus rex is that it was a big dinosaur that lived 65 to 85 million years ago. The rest is just guessing. That's what is so exciting. Someone might discover something next week, next year, or in twenty years' time that tells us a whole lot more. And who knows? It might just be you!

T. REX
EXHIBITION

OPENS TODAY!

MU